# Kids Can Draw
# ANCIENT EGYPT

by Philippe Legendre

*Walter Foster*

© 2002 Groupe Fleurus-Mame, Paris.
Text on pages 4–24 © 2002 Walter Foster Publishing, Inc. All rights reserved.
Original title *J'apprends à dessiner l'Égypte,* © 1998 Groupe Fleurus-Mame, Paris.

## Attention Parents and Teachers

All children can draw a circle, a square, or a triangle . . . which means that they can also learn to draw a sphinx, boat on the Nile, or King Tutankhamen! The KIDS CAN DRAW learning method is easy and fun. Children will learn a technique and a vocabulary of shapes that will form the basis for all kinds of drawing.

Pictures are created by combining geometric shapes to form a mass of volumes and surfaces. From this stage, children can give character to their sketches with straight, curved, or broken lines.

With just a few strokes of the pencil, an Egyptian scene will appear—and with the addition of color, the picture will be real work of art!

The KIDS CAN DRAW method offers a real apprenticeship in technique and a first look at composition, proportion, shapes, and lines. The simplicity of this method ensures that the pleasure of drawing is always the most important factor.

## About Philippe Legendre

French painter, engraver, and illustrator, Philippe Legendre also runs a school of art for children aged 6–14 years. Legendre frequently spends time in schools and has developed this method of learning so that all children can discover the artist within themselves.

# Helpful Tips

1. Each picture is made up of simple geometric shapes, which are illustrated at the top of the left-hand page. This is called the **Vocabulary of Shapes.** Encourage children to practice drawing each shape before starting their pictures.

2. Suggest children use a pencil to do their sketches. This way, if they don't like a particular shape, they can just erase it and try again.

3. A dotted line indicates that the line should be erased. Have children draw the whole shape and then erase the dotted part of the line.

4. Once children finish their drawings, they can color them with crayons, colored pencils, or felt-tip markers. They may want to go over the lines with a black pencil or pen.

## Now let's get started!

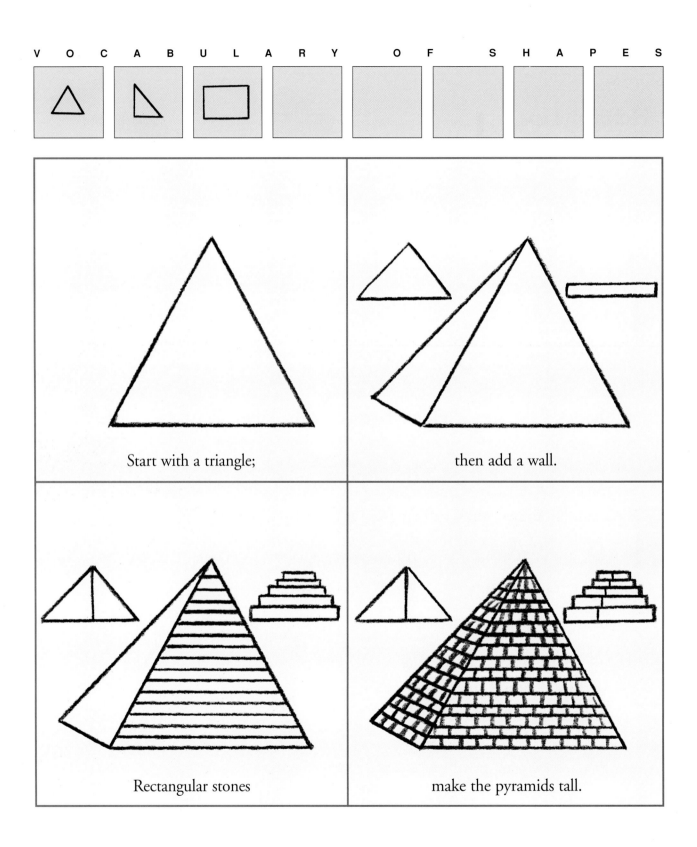

Start with a triangle;

then add a wall.

Rectangular stones

make the pyramids tall.

# Pyramids

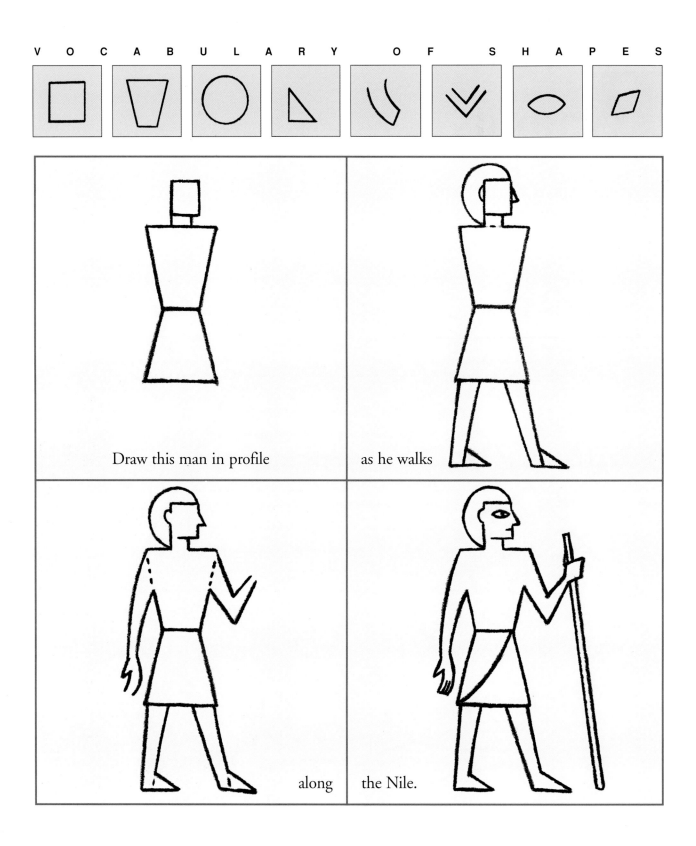

Draw this man in profile

as he walks

along

the Nile.

# **E**gyptian Man

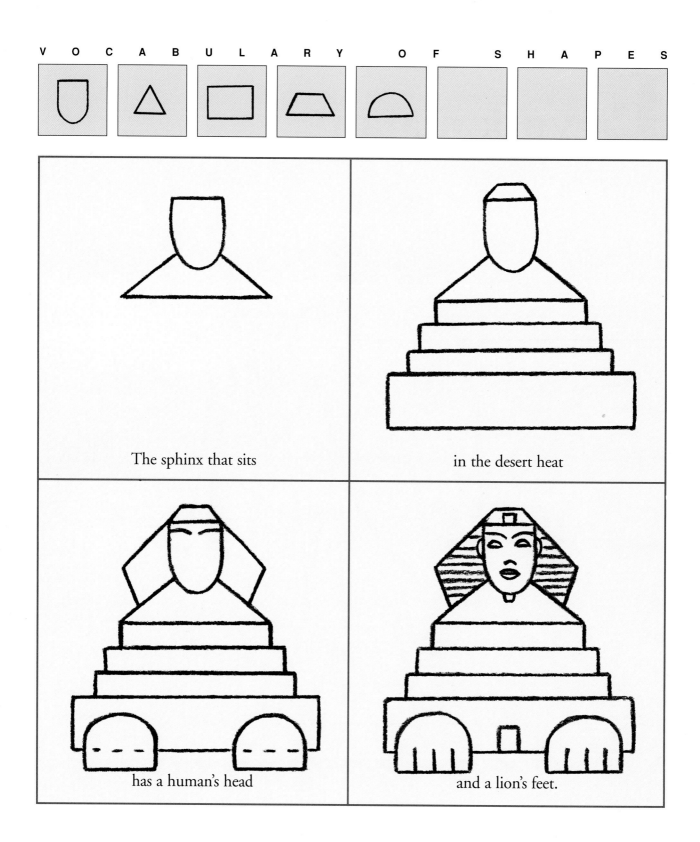

The sphinx that sits

in the desert heat

has a human's head

and a lion's feet.

# Sphinx

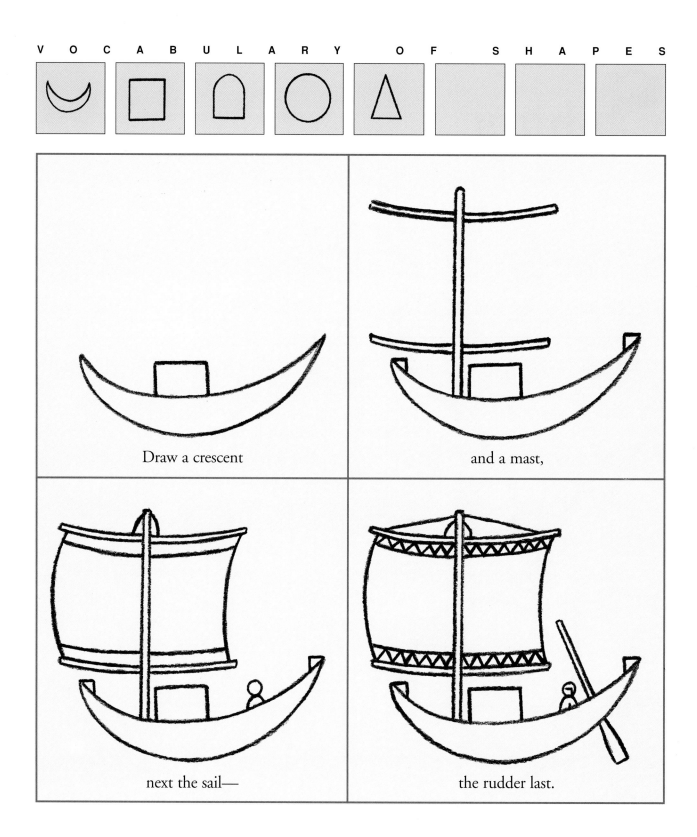

Draw a crescent

and a mast,

next the sail—

the rudder last.

# Boat on the Nile

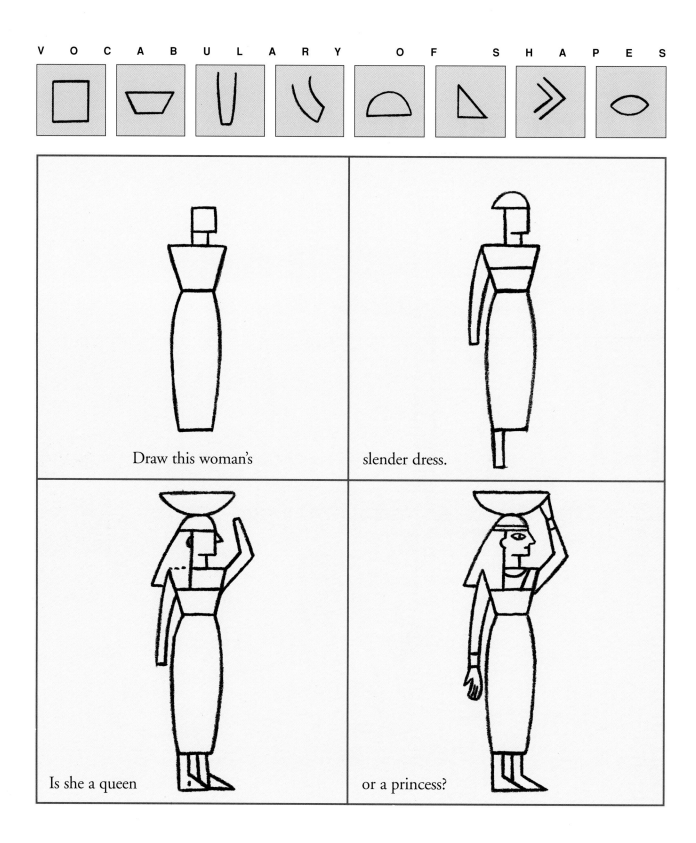

Draw this woman's

slender dress.

Is she a queen

or a princess?

# **E**gyptian Woman

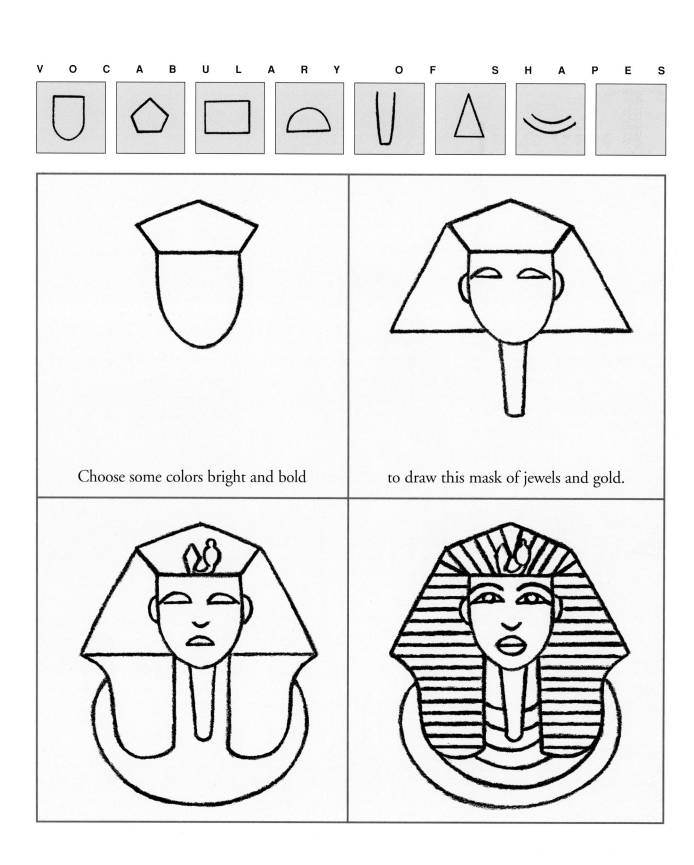

Choose some colors bright and bold

to draw this mask of jewels and gold.

# Tutankhamen

This king of Egypt's

hat is blue.

On each foot's

a golden shoe.

# Pharaoh

Draw two big circles on one square block.

The sun god Ra has the head of a hawk.

# Ra

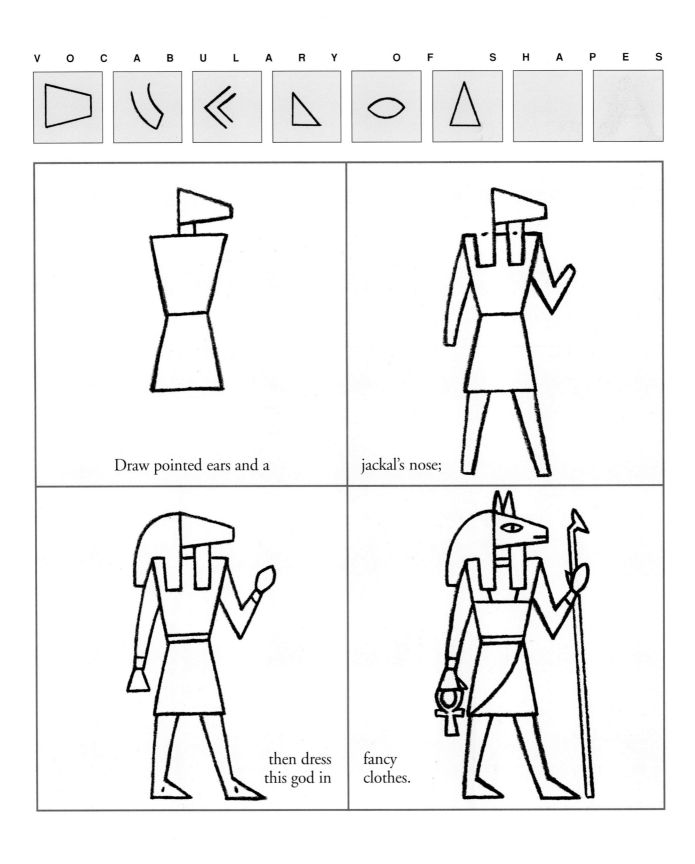

Draw pointed ears and a

jackal's nose;

then dress this god in

fancy clothes.

# Anubis

In Egypt, they lived and played under the sun.

Now draw your own scene. Be creative! Have fun!